GIANTS™

MAD LIBS®

by Michael T. Riley

Mad Libs
An Imprint of Penguin Random House

MAD LIBS
Penguin Young Readers Group
An Imprint of Penguin Random House LLC

Concept created by Roger Price & Leonard Stern

Published by Mad Libs,
an imprint of Penguin Random House LLC,
345 Hudson Street, New York, New York 10014.
Printed in the USA.

ISBN 9780451534460
1 3 5 7 9 10 8 6 4 2

MAD LIBS

INSTRUCTIONS

MAD LIBS® is a game for people who don't like games! It can be played by one, two, three, four, or forty.

• RIDICULOUSLY SIMPLE DIRECTIONS

In this tablet you will find stories containing blank spaces where words are left out. One player, the READER, selects one of these stories. The READER does not tell anyone what the story is about. Instead, he/she asks the other players, the WRITERS, to give him/her words. These words are used to fill in the blank spaces in the story.

• TO PLAY

The READER asks each WRITER in turn to call out a word—an adjective or a noun or whatever the space calls for—and uses them to fill in the blank spaces in the story. The result is a MAD LIBS® game.

When the READER then reads the completed MAD LIBS® game to the other players, they will discover that they have written a story that is fantastic, screamingly funny, shocking, silly, crazy, or just plain dumb—depending upon which words each WRITER called out.

• EXAMPLE (*Before* and *After*)

"_____!" he said _____
    EXCLAMATION   ADVERB

as he jumped into his convertible _____ and
                                         NOUN

drove off with his _____ wife.
                        ADJECTIVE

"_____OUCH_____!" he said _____STUPIDLY_____
    EXCLAMATION   ADVERB

as he jumped into his convertible _____CAT_____ and
                                         NOUN

drove off with his _____BRAVE_____ wife.
                        ADJECTIVE

MAD LIBS®
QUICK REVIEW

In case you have forgotten what adjectives, adverbs, nouns, and verbs are, here is a quick review:

An ADJECTIVE describes something or somebody. *Lumpy, soft, ugly, messy,* and *short* are adjectives.

An ADVERB tells how something is done. It modifies a verb and usually ends in "ly." *Modestly, stupidly, greedily,* and *carefully* are adverbs.

A NOUN is the name of a person, place, or thing. *Sidewalk, umbrella, bridle, bathtub,* and *nose* are nouns.

A VERB is an action word. *Run, pitch, jump,* and *swim* are verbs. Put the verbs in past tense if the directions say PAST TENSE. *Ran, pitched, jumped,* and *swam* are verbs in the past tense.

When we ask for A PLACE, we mean any sort of place: a country or city (*Spain, Cleveland*) or a room (*bathroom, kitchen*).

An EXCLAMATION or SILLY WORD is any sort of funny sound, gasp, grunt, or outcry, like *Wow!, Ouch!, Whomp!, Ick!,* and *Gadzooks!*

When we ask for specific words, like a NUMBER, a COLOR, an ANIMAL, or a PART OF THE BODY, we mean a word that is one of those things, like *seven, blue, horse,* or *head.*

When we ask for a PLURAL, it means more than one. For example, *cat* pluralized is *cats.*

MAD LIBS® is fun to play with friends, but you can also play it by yourself! To begin with, DO NOT look at the story on the page below. Fill in the blanks on this page with the words called for. Then, using the words you have selected, fill in the blank spaces in the story.

Now you've created your own hilarious MAD LIBS® game!

MEET THE GIANTS: BUSTER POSEY

NOUN _____

PLURAL NOUN _____

PART OF THE BODY _____

ADJECTIVE _____

NOUN _____

VERB (PAST TENSE) _____

NOUN _____

ADJECTIVE _____

ADJECTIVE _____

NOUN _____

PLURAL NOUN _____

NOUN _____

ADJECTIVE _____

NOUN _____

TYPE OF LIQUID _____

VERB ENDING IN "ING" _____

NOUN _____

VERB ENDING IN "ING" _____

MAD LIBS®
MEET THE GIANTS:
BUSTER POSEY

Since becoming the fifth overall _____ selected in the 2008
                                    NOUN

First-Year Player Draft, Buster Posey has carried the _____
                                                        PLURAL NOUN

of an entire city on his _____. The Giants knew they made
                          PART OF THE BODY

a/an _____ choice in 2010 when Posey claimed the National
      ADJECTIVE

League _____ of the Year Award and _____
        NOUN   VERB (PAST TENSE)

every _____ during their _____ playoff run.
       NOUN   ADJECTIVE

While defending his first World Series ring, a/an _____
                                                    ADJECTIVE

collision with a/an _____ resulted in Posey's walking on
                     NOUN

_____ for several months. Amazingly, Posey returned
PLURAL NOUN

even better and became the first catcher since Johnny Bench, of the

famed "Big Red _____," to win the National League's Most
                NOUN

_____ _____ Award. Over three championship
ADJECTIVE   NOUN

seasons, Buster has been the _____ that keeps the
                              TYPE OF LIQUID

Giants' engine _____. He has also been behind the
                VERB ENDING IN "ING"

_____ for three no-hitters, making him a popular target for
NOUN

the team's _____ staff.
            VERB ENDING IN "ING"

From SAN FRANCISCO GIANTS MAD LIBS® • ™ and © Major League Baseball Properties, Inc.
Published in 2017 by Mad Libs, an imprint of Penguin Random House LLC.

MAD LIBS® is fun to play with friends, but you can also play it by yourself! To begin with, DO NOT look at the story on the page below. Fill in the blanks on this page with the words called for. Then, using the words you have selected, fill in the blank spaces in the story.

Now you've created your own hilarious MAD LIBS® game!

THE BIRTH OF A DYNASTY: 2010

NOUN _____

NUMBER _____

NOUN _____

PART OF THE BODY _____

ADJECTIVE _____

PLURAL NOUN _____

VERB ENDING IN "ING" _____

PLURAL NOUN _____

PLURAL NOUN _____

ADJECTIVE _____

ADJECTIVE _____

TYPE OF LIQUID _____

OCCUPATION _____

PART OF THE BODY _____

NOUN _____

NOUN _____

A PLACE _____

MAD LIBS
THE BIRTH OF A
DYNASTY: 2010

Emotions swung like a/an _____ during the 2010 season.
<u>NOUN</u>

The Giants went from walking on cloud _____ to experiencing
<u>NUMBER</u>

a series of defeats that felt like a/an _____ right in the
<u>NOUN</u>

_____. Broadcasters called it "torture" because fans became so
<u>PART OF THE BODY</u>

_____ that they had to breathe into paper _____
<u>ADJECTIVE</u>   <u>PLURAL NOUN</u>

to keep from _____! No one expected to play for all
<u>VERB ENDING IN "ING"</u>

the _____ in October, especially with a roster lovingly
<u>PLURAL NOUN</u>

referred to as a bunch of _____. But the Giants rallied
<u>PLURAL NOUN</u>

behind a/an _____ starting rotation of Tim Lincecum, Matt
<u>ADJECTIVE</u>

Cain, and Jonathan Sanchez, and a lineup all but stuck together with

_____ _____. Even closer Brian Wilson looked
<u>ADJECTIVE</u>   <u>TYPE OF LIQUID</u>

like a royal _____ with his long, dark _____. With
<u>OCCUPATION</u>   <u>PART OF THE BODY</u>

Aubrey Huff modeling a rally _____ and clutch hitting by
<u>NOUN</u>

Cody Ross, the Giants captured their first _____ since they left
<u>NOUN</u>

(the) _____ for the Bay.
<u>A PLACE</u>

From SAN FRANCISCO GIANTS MAD LIBS® • ™ and © Major League Baseball Properties, Inc.
Published in 2017 by Mad Libs, an imprint of Penguin Random House LLC.

MAD LIBS® is fun to play with friends, but you can also play it by yourself! To begin with, DO NOT look at the story on the page below. Fill in the blanks on this page with the words called for. Then, using the words you have selected, fill in the blank spaces in the story.

Now you've created your own hilarious MAD LIBS® game!

HOW SWEEP IT IS: 2012

ADJECTIVE _____

ADJECTIVE _____

NOUN _____

ADJECTIVE _____

PLURAL NOUN _____

ADJECTIVE _____

NOUN _____

NOUN _____

PLURAL NOUN _____

ADJECTIVE _____

NOUN _____

PART OF THE BODY _____

ANIMAL _____

PLURAL NOUN _____

NOUN _____

NOUN _____

PLURAL NOUN _____

Whoever said it's not over until the _____ lady sings was

ADJECTIVE

talking about the 2012 Giants. This _____ bunch never saw

ADJECTIVE

a/an _____ too _____ to climb. Trailing by two

NOUN   ADJECTIVE

_____ in both the NLDS and NLCS, they remained

PLURAL NOUN

_____ and took it one _____ at a time. Barry Zito

ADJECTIVE   NOUN

delivered his best start since crossing the _____ Bridge from

NOUN

the Oakland _____ to help propel the team back to the

PLURAL NOUN

World Series. Considered _____ underdogs against the Tigers

ADJECTIVE

and Triple _____ winner Miguel Cabrera, the Giants did not

NOUN

blink a/an _____. Pablo "Kung Fu _____" Sandoval

PART OF THE BODY   ANIMAL

clubbed three homers in Game 1 to set the _____ in

PLURAL NOUN

motion. Gutsy pitching by Ryan Vogelsong and closer Sergio Romo

kept Detroit's bats under lock and _____. With a 3-0 series

NOUN

lead, Marco Scutaro caught the final _____ in Game 4, and it

NOUN

was time to break out the _____ for the sweep!

PLURAL NOUN

MAD LIBS® is fun to play with friends, but you can also play it by yourself! To begin with, DO NOT look at the story on the page below. Fill in the blanks on this page with the words called for. Then, using the words you have selected, fill in the blank spaces in the story.

Now you've created your own hilarious MAD LIBS® game!

GIANTS LEGENDS: WILLIE MAYS

NOUN _____

NOUN _____

EXCLAMATION _____

PLURAL NOUN _____

NOUN _____

PLURAL NOUN _____

VERB ENDING IN "ING" _____

PART OF THE BODY (PLURAL) _____

NOUN _____

PLURAL NOUN _____

VERB _____

NOUN _____

NOUN _____

PART OF THE BODY _____

NOUN _____

PLURAL NOUN _____

NOUN _____

NOUN _____

Willie Mays is more than a first-_____ Hall of Famer. The
NOUN

Hall could probably add another _____ to the building
NOUN

dedicated to the "Say _____ Kid." Mays did it all. When he
EXCLAMATION

wasn't sending one of his 660 _____ sailing into the upper
PLURAL NOUN

_____, he was collecting more than 3,000 _____,
NOUN   PLURAL NOUN

and _____ so fast his _____ never
VERB ENDING IN "ING"   PART OF THE BODY (PLURAL)

touched the _____. In center field, his territory was where
NOUN

extra base _____ went to _____. In the 1954
PLURAL NOUN   VERB

World Series, he made arguably the most famous _____ of
NOUN

all time while sprinting toward the outfield _____ with his
NOUN

_____ completely turned! Today, AT&T Park's entrance is
PART OF THE BODY

named Willie Mays _____, and Mays has been presented
NOUN

with too many honorary _____ to count, such as the
PLURAL NOUN

Presidential _____ of Freedom. Willie Mays is not just a
NOUN

baseball legend, he is a national _____!
NOUN

MAD LIBS® is fun to play with friends, but you can also play it by yourself! To begin with, DO NOT look at the story on the page below. Fill in the blanks on this page with the words called for. Then, using the words you have selected, fill in the blank spaces in the story.

Now you've created your own hilarious MAD LIBS® game!

KNOW YOUR RIVAL: THE LOS ANGELES DODGERS

NOUN _____

PLURAL NOUN _____

PLURAL NOUN _____

NOUN _____

PLURAL NOUN _____

ADJECTIVE _____

TYPE OF LIQUID _____

COLOR _____

CELEBRITY _____

ARTICLE OF CLOTHING _____

PERSON IN ROOM _____

PLURAL NOUN _____

PLURAL NOUN _____

PLURAL NOUN _____

NOUN _____

NOUN _____

MAD LIBS
KNOW YOUR RIVAL: THE LOS ANGELES DODGERS

With a name inspired by the term "_____ Dodgers," an
NOUN

insult poking fun at trolley _____ posing danger to
PLURAL NOUN

_____ walking around the team's original home in
PLURAL NOUN

Brooklyn, the Dodgers are the Giants' biggest _____. When
NOUN

both teams packed their _____ to leave New York for
PLURAL NOUN

the _____ California sunshine, the bad _____
ADJECTIVE   TYPE OF LIQUID

between them only intensified. The Dodgers represent Hollywood,

where tabloids flock to _____ carpet premieres to catch a
COLOR

glimpse of _____ wearing the latest _____
CELEBRITY   ARTICLE OF CLOTHING

designed by _____. San Francisco does not have as many
PERSON IN ROOM

A-list _____ walking around, but it is still a proud city,
PLURAL NOUN

especially when beating the _____ out of opposing
PLURAL NOUN

_____ such as Clayton Kershaw, Yasiel Puig, and Adrian
PLURAL NOUN

Gonzalez. A Giants-Dodgers game is always reason to be on the edge

of your _____, knowing you might see a/an _____
NOUN   NOUN

that makes history.

MAD LIBS® is fun to play with friends, but you can also play it by yourself! To begin with, DO NOT look at the story on the page below. Fill in the blanks on this page with the words called for. Then, using the words you have selected, fill in the blank spaces in the story.

Now you've created your own hilarious MAD LIBS® game!

HOME SWEET HOME

ADJECTIVE _____

NOUN _____

PLURAL NOUN _____

PLURAL NOUN _____

NOUN _____

ADJECTIVE _____

PLURAL NOUN _____

NOUN _____

NOUN _____

TYPE OF LIQUID _____

PLURAL NOUN _____

NOUN _____

PLURAL NOUN _____

SILLY WORD _____

ADJECTIVE _____

ANIMAL _____

ANIMAL _____

PLURAL NOUN _____

MAD LIBS®
HOME SWEET HOME

Located along the _____ shore of the San Francisco
                        ADJECTIVE

_____, AT&T Park is the home of the Giants. With its many
   NOUN

state-of-the-art _____ and breathtaking _____,
                  PLURAL NOUN   PLURAL NOUN

it is a destination for any fan to include on his or her _____
                                                          NOUN

list. Though its _____ _____ give pitchers an
                 ADJECTIVE   PLURAL NOUN

advantage, it is one of the best venues to witness a home run. When a

Giants batter smashes one, fans hear a blaring _____ sound as
                                                NOUN

a massive Coca-Cola _____ lights up and _____
                     NOUN   TYPE OF LIQUID

shoots into the sky. Homers that sail over the _____ atop
                                                PLURAL NOUN

the right-field wall land in McCovey _____, where fans float
                                      NOUN

around in _____ waiting to claim a "_____ hit" as a
           PLURAL NOUN   SILLY WORD

souvenir. If all this excitement makes you _____, AT&T Park
                                            ADJECTIVE

serves some of the best _____ chowder and _____
                         ANIMAL   ANIMAL

sandwiches in all of baseball. Make sure to try their famous garlic

_____, which can be smelled throughout the ballpark!
   PLURAL NOUN

From SAN FRANCISCO GIANTS MAD LIBS® • ™ and © Major League Baseball Properties, Inc.
Published in 2017 by Mad Libs, an imprint of Penguin Random House LLC.

MAD LIBS® is fun to play with friends, but you can also play it by yourself! To begin with, DO NOT look at the story on the page below. Fill in the blanks on this page with the words called for. Then, using the words you have selected, fill in the blank spaces in the story.

Now you've created your own hilarious MAD LIBS® game!

GIANTS LEGENDS: WILLIE MCCOVEY

OCCUPATION (PLURAL) _____

ADJECTIVE _____

ADJECTIVE _____

PART OF THE BODY (PLURAL) _____

CELEBRITY _____

NOUN _____

PLURAL NOUN _____

NOUN _____

NOUN _____

NOUN _____

NOUN _____

ADVERB _____

SILLY WORD _____

NOUN _____

FIRST NAME (MALE) _____

NOUN _____

MAD LIBS®
GIANTS LEGENDS:
WILLIE MCCOVEY

No one made National League _____ more _____
                                 OCCUPATION (PLURAL)   ADJECTIVE

than Willie McCovey. Nicknamed "Stretch" for his amazingly

_____ _____, McCovey was a natural first
   ADJECTIVE   PART OF THE BODY (PLURAL)

baseman, but he is revered for his home runs, which a manager once

described as an act of _____. He wore number 44 in honor
                          CELEBRITY

of Hank Aaron and eventually joined Hank in the 500 _____
                                                         NOUN

Club. McCovey often cleared the _____ at the old
                                    PLURAL NOUN

Candlestick _____ with one powerful _____, which
                NOUN   NOUN

inspired the Giants to name the _____ behind AT&T
                                    NOUN

_____ after him. More imposing, however, were his line
   NOUN

drives that shot through the infield so _____ they made a/an
                                            ADVERB

" _____ " sound like a/an _____ shot out of a cannon.
   SILLY WORD   NOUN

McCovey shared the name, _____, with his teammate
                              FIRST NAME (MALE)

Willie Mays and also has a bronze _____ outside the stadium.
                                      NOUN

From SAN FRANCISCO GIANTS MAD LIBS® • ™ and © Major League Baseball Properties, Inc.
Published in 2017 by Mad Libs, an imprint of Penguin Random House LLC.

MAD LIBS® is fun to play with friends, but you can also play it by yourself! To begin with, DO NOT look at the story on the page below. Fill in the blanks on this page with the words called for. Then, using the words you have selected, fill in the blank spaces in the story.

Now you've created your own hilarious MAD LIBS® game!

MATT CAIN'S PERFECT GAME

NOUN _____

PLURAL NOUN _____

PLURAL NOUN _____

NOUN _____

A PLACE _____

OCCUPATION _____

NOUN _____

NOUN _____

ADJECTIVE _____

VERB (PAST TENSE) _____

PLURAL NOUN _____

PLURAL NOUN _____

A PLACE _____

PART OF THE BODY (PLURAL) _____

NOUN _____

NOUN _____

VERB ENDING IN "ING" _____

PART OF THE BODY (PLURAL) _____

MAD LIBS®
MATT CAIN'S
PERFECT GAME

To pitch a perfect _____, you must not only surrender zero

NOUN

_____, you must also face twenty-seven _____

PLURAL NOUN   PLURAL NOUN

without allowing a/an _____ to reach (the) _____

NOUN   A PLACE

safely. Until 2012, no Giants _____ had done this. That

OCCUPATION

year, Matt Cain was the _____ of the staff and on June

NOUN

13 was at the top of his _____. Fans sensed it would be

NOUN

a/an _____ night when Cain easily _____

ADJECTIVE   VERB (PAST TENSE)

the first two _____ he saw. Fourteen of the Houston

PLURAL NOUN

_____ went down the same way, walking back to

PLURAL NOUN

(the) _____ shaking their _____ in

A PLACE   PART OF THE BODY (PLURAL)

frustration. When they made contact, Lady _____ was on

NOUN

Cain's side. Melky Cabrera and Gregor Blanco saved the _____

NOUN

with spectacular plays at the _____ track. When Cain

VERB ENDING IN "ING"

became only the twenty-second pitcher in history to toss a perfecto,

fans rejoiced at the top of their _____!

PART OF THE BODY (PLURAL)

From SAN FRANCISCO GIANTS MAD LIBS® • ™ and © Major League Baseball Properties, Inc.
Published in 2017 by Mad Libs, an imprint of Penguin Random House LLC.

MAD LIBS® is fun to play with friends, but you can also play it by yourself! To begin with, DO NOT look at the story on the page below. Fill in the blanks on this page with the words called for. Then, using the words you have selected, fill in the blank spaces in the story.

Now you've created your own hilarious MAD LIBS® game!

MEET THE GIANTS: MADISON BUMGARNER

PLURAL NOUN _____

VERB _____

PLURAL NOUN _____

ADJECTIVE _____

NOUN _____

NOUN _____

NOUN _____

VERB _____

PLURAL NOUN _____

NOUN _____

NOUN _____

ADJECTIVE _____

PART OF THE BODY _____

LAST NAME _____

VERB ENDING IN "ING" _____

SILLY WORD _____

VERB _____

NOUN _____

MAD LIBS
MEET THE GIANTS:
MADISON BUMGARNER

Madison Bumgarner was not even old enough to buy _____
                                                      PLURAL NOUN

during his 2010 rookie year, but he could still _____ one of the
                                                      VERB

biggest _____ in Giants history. His eight _____
          PLURAL NOUN   ADJECTIVE

innings in Game 4 of the World Series gave the team the _____
                                                              NOUN

it needed to bring the Golden City its first-ever _____.
                                                        NOUN

Bumgarner's _____ in the Bay Area has done nothing but
                NOUN

_____ since then. Pitching in all three _____, he's
   VERB   PLURAL NOUN

been a/an _____ in the Giants' recent _____. His
             NOUN   NOUN

_____ performance in Game 7 of the 2014 World Series may
  ADJECTIVE

have earned his _____ a spot on the Mount _____
                  PART OF THE BODY   LAST NAME

of Giants legends, and he is not through _____ by
                                            VERB ENDING IN "ING"

a long shot. What is even scarier (if you are an LA _____
                                                        SILLY WORD

fan) is that Bumgarner can also _____ better than some
                                    VERB

position players. Who knows? Maybe he'll be the first pitcher to win

the _____ Derby!
       NOUN

From SAN FRANCISCO GIANTS MAD LIBS® • ™ and © Major League Baseball Properties, Inc.
Published in 2017 by Mad Libs, an imprint of Penguin Random House LLC.

MAD LIBS® is fun to play with friends, but you can also play it by yourself! To begin with, DO NOT look at the story on the page below. Fill in the blanks on this page with the words called for. Then, using the words you have selected, fill in the blank spaces in the story.

Now you've created your own hilarious MAD LIBS® game!

MUST BE THE
EVEN YEARS: 2014

NOUN _____

PLURAL NOUN _____

VERB (PAST TENSE) _____

NOUN _____

NOUN _____

ADJECTIVE _____

PLURAL NOUN _____

ADJECTIVE _____

PART OF THE BODY _____

NOUN _____

NOUN _____

NOUN _____

ADJECTIVE _____

NOUN _____

NOUN _____

ADJECTIVE _____

PLURAL NOUN _____

NOUN _____

MAD LIBS®
MUST BE THE
EVEN YEARS: 2014

After a third-_____ finish in 2013, the Giants rebounded in
_{NOUN}

2014 to continue their pattern of reaching the Fall Classic during even-

numbered _____. Their third World Series appearance in six
_{PLURAL NOUN}

years was the most tightly _____, with the Giants and Royals
_{VERB (PAST TENSE)}

tied at two games apiece. Heading into Game 5, Madison Bumgarner

tossed a complete _____ without allowing Kansas City a single
_{NOUN}

_____. It was a/an _____ performance, but Bumgarner
_{NOUN} _{ADJECTIVE}

was not done leaving his mark in the history _____. With
_{PLURAL NOUN}

only two days to give his _____ left _____ some
_{ADJECTIVE} _{PART OF THE BODY}

rest, he heroically entered _____ 7 in relief. After another
_{NOUN}

key _____ from unsung _____ Jeremy Affeldt and
_{NOUN} _{NOUN}

a/an _____ defensive play by rookie Joe Panik, manager Bruce
_{ADJECTIVE}

Bochy gave Bumgarner the _____. Clinging to a one-run
_{NOUN}

lead, the Giants' ace shut the _____ on the Royals' lineup for a
_{NOUN}

historic World Series save. His five _____ _____ put
_{ADJECTIVE} _{PLURAL NOUN}

the finishing touches on the team's most satisfying _____ yet!
_{NOUN}

From SAN FRANCISCO GIANTS MAD LIBS® • ™ and © Major League Baseball Properties, Inc.
Published in 2017 by Mad Libs, an imprint of Penguin Random House LLC.

MAD LIBS® is fun to play with friends, but you can also play it by yourself! To begin with, DO NOT look at the story on the page below. Fill in the blanks on this page with the words called for. Then, using the words you have selected, fill in the blank spaces in the story.

Now you've created your own hilarious MAD LIBS® game!

ORIGINS: THE NEW YORK GIANTS

TYPE OF FOOD _____

ADJECTIVE _____

SILLY WORD _____

NOUN _____

A PLACE _____

VERB ENDING IN "ING" _____

ADJECTIVE _____

NOUN _____

SAME NOUN _____

NOUN _____

PART OF THE BODY (PLURAL) _____

ADJECTIVE _____

ADJECTIVE _____

NUMBER _____

ADJECTIVE _____

NOUN _____

MAD LIBS
ORIGINS: THE
NEW YORK GIANTS

The original Giants played in the city known as the Big _____

TYPE OF FOOD

in the _____ section of Manhattan. Their home ballpark, the

ADJECTIVE

_____ Grounds, was where Bobby Thomson hit the famous

SILLY WORD

"_____ heard 'round (the) _____." Thomson's blast

NOUN _A PLACE_

left the Brooklyn Dodgers _____ on the field feeling

VERB ENDING IN "ING"

_____ while the announcer shouted, "The Giants win the

ADJECTIVE

_____! The Giants win the _____!" Despite their

NOUN _SAME NOUN_

success, the team moved west seeking a new _____. New

NOUN

Yorkers were left with broken _____, but their

PART OF THE BODY (PLURAL)

_____ loss was San Francisco's gain! The Giants kept their

ADJECTIVE

_____ uniform colors and switched the "NY" logo to an "SF,"

ADJECTIVE

like the city's football team, the _____-ers. Around the same

NUMBER

time, the Dodgers moved to LA, allowing the _____ rivalry to

ADJECTIVE

continue. New York would later add the Mets as an expansion team,

giving the Giants a chance to fly east for a homecoming _____

NOUN

every year.

MAD LIBS® is fun to play with friends, but you can also play it by yourself! To begin with, DO NOT look at the story on the page below. Fill in the blanks on this page with the words called for. Then, using the words you have selected, fill in the blank spaces in the story.

Now you've created your own hilarious MAD LIBS® game!

GIANTS LEGENDS: JUAN MARICHAL

VERB ENDING IN "ING" _____

PLURAL NOUN _____

PLURAL NOUN _____

PLURAL NOUN _____

NOUN _____

ADJECTIVE _____

NOUN _____

PART OF THE BODY _____

OCCUPATION (PLURAL) _____

PART OF THE BODY _____

PERSON IN ROOM _____

SILLY WORD _____

PLURAL NOUN _____

PLURAL NOUN _____

PLURAL NOUN _____

VERB ENDING IN "ING" _____

PLURAL NOUN _____

NOUN _____

MAD LIBS
GIANTS LEGENDS:
JUAN MARICHAL

As a child, Juan Marichal practiced _____ using
_{VERB ENDING IN "ING"}

taped-up _____ for baseballs. In the Majors, this
_{PLURAL NOUN}

Dominican-born hurler baffled _____ and used
_{PLURAL NOUN}

intimidation _____ to keep hitters uncomfortable at
_{PLURAL NOUN}

the _____. His _____ windup was pictured on
_{NOUN}   _{ADJECTIVE}

a 1966 cover of _____ magazine with a banner that read,
_{NOUN}

"The Best Right _____ in Baseball"—and most
_{PART OF THE BODY}

_____ would agree. Before each pitch, Marichal would
_{OCCUPATION (PLURAL)}

thrust his _____ high into the air like martial arts master
_{PART OF THE BODY}

_____ performing a deadly _____ kick. This unusual
_{PERSON IN ROOM}   _{SILLY WORD}

motion earned him more _____ in the 1960s than any
_{PLURAL NOUN}

other pitcher. Of his 244 complete _____, one stands out.
_{PLURAL NOUN}

Both Marichal and Warren Spahn surrendered zero _____
_{PLURAL NOUN}

while _____ until the sixteenth inning! This legendary
_{VERB ENDING IN "ING"}

Hall of Famer paved the way for Giants pitcher Johnny Cueto and

other Dominican _____, and has had his _____
_{PLURAL NOUN}   _{NOUN}

retired by the Giants.

MAD LIBS® is fun to play with friends, but you can also play it by yourself! To begin with, DO NOT look at the story on the page below. Fill in the blanks on this page with the words called for. Then, using the words you have selected, fill in the blank spaces in the story.

Now you've created your own hilarious MAD LIBS® game!

MEET THE GIANTS: HUNTER PENCE

VERB _____

PLURAL NOUN _____

NOUN _____

NOUN _____

PART OF THE BODY _____

NOUN _____

NOUN _____

TYPE OF FOOD _____

ADJECTIVE _____

ADJECTIVE _____

NOUN _____

A PLACE _____

NOUN _____

NOUN _____

NOUN _____

EXCLAMATION _____

As team leader, Hunter Pence always gets his teammates ready to

_____ with his fiery _____ of encouragement.
    VERB   PLURAL NOUN

Pence is nicknamed "The _____" for his ability to hold
                                  NOUN

a/an _____ in the palm of his _____. Listeners hang
         NOUN   PART OF THE BODY

on to every _____ Pence delivers and would run through a
                 NOUN

brick _____ for him. They even show their love by showering
         NOUN

him with packs of salty _____ seeds. Pence's _____
                TYPE OF FOOD   ADJECTIVE

style and attitude have made him a cult figure, and his _____
                                  ADJECTIVE

hitting and willingness to sacrifice his _____ to make a catch
                           NOUN

have made him a San Francisco hero. Pence arrived in a trade from

(the) _____ in 2012. During that year's NLCS, he defied physics
     A PLACE

by striking the _____ three times with one _____!
                 NOUN   NOUN

At the plate, in the dugout, or even just flashing his _____
                                         NOUN

in the Bay Area, Pence has a knack for inspiring jubilant chants of

_____!
  EXCLAMATION

MAD LIBS® is fun to play with friends, but you can also play it by yourself! To begin with, DO NOT look at the story on the page below. Fill in the blanks on this page with the words called for. Then, using the words you have selected, fill in the blank spaces in the story.

Now you've created your own hilarious MAD LIBS® game!

I LOVE THE '90S

NOUN _____

A PLACE _____

ADJECTIVE _____

PLURAL NOUN _____

PLURAL NOUN _____

OCCUPATION _____

NOUN _____

PART OF THE BODY _____

ADJECTIVE _____

ANIMAL _____

PLURAL NOUN _____

PLURAL NOUN _____

NOUN _____

The decade that produced the World Wide _____ and *The Fresh*

NOUN

Prince of (the) _____ also featured several celebrated ballplayers

A PLACE

by the Bay. Please be kind and rewind to these Giants classics:

Matt Williams: This fan favorite manned the "_____ corner"

ADJECTIVE

and picked up four Gold _____ as a third baseman.

PLURAL NOUN

Jeff Kent: Kent enjoyed his best _____ in the City by the

PLURAL NOUN

Bay and has recently returned as a/an _____.

OCCUPATION

Kevin Mitchell: This former MVP once saved a/an _____ by

NOUN

making a catch with his bare _____!

PART OF THE BODY

Robby Thompson: As scrappy as a/an _____ _____,

ADJECTIVE   ANIMAL

Thompson was pesky on opposing _____.

PLURAL NOUN

Robb Nen: Nen replaced Rod Beck as closer and broke Beck's record

for most _____ in team history.

PLURAL NOUN

Will Clark: "Will The Thrill" helped the Giants claim the National

League _____ in 1989.

NOUN

MAD LIBS® is fun to play with friends, but you can also play it by yourself! To begin with, DO NOT look at the story on the page below. Fill in the blanks on this page with the words called for. Then, using the words you have selected, fill in the blank spaces in the story.

Now you've created your own hilarious MAD LIBS® game!

CELEBRITY GIANTS FANS

TYPE OF FOOD _____

TYPE OF LIQUID _____

ADJECTIVE _____

PLURAL NOUN _____

ADJECTIVE _____

PLURAL NOUN _____

NOUN _____

ADJECTIVE _____

VERB _____

PLURAL NOUN _____

VERB _____

NOUN _____

VERB ENDING IN "ING" _____

MAD LIBS®
CELEBRITY
GIANTS FANS

You never know who might be waiting in the fried _____ line
                                                    TYPE OF FOOD

at AT&T Park. If you see these celebrities, offer them an ice-cold bottle

of _____ for an autograph!
      TYPE OF LIQUID

Danny Glover: This _____ celebrity has a trailer filled with
                            ADJECTIVE

collectible Giants _____.
                       PLURAL NOUN

Zooey Deschanel: The star of _____ Girl and *(500)* _____
                                    ADJECTIVE   PLURAL NOUN

of Summer spends her own summers repping black and orange.

Bob Saget: This comedian flaunted his fandom as a TV dad on the

sitcom *Full* _____.
               NOUN

Rob Schneider: This *Saturday Night* _____ alum likes to
                                             ADJECTIVE

holler, "You can _____ it!"
                    VERB

James Hetfield: What gets Metallica's front man psyched? Playing his

Master of _____ album while watching a Giants reliever
                PLURAL NOUN

_____ another _____ in the ninth.
   VERB   NOUN

Steve Perry: This '80s rocker journeys to the ballgame to remind fellow

fans to "Don't Stop _____."
                       VERB ENDING IN "ING"

MAD LIBS® is fun to play with friends, but you can also play it by yourself! To begin with, DO NOT look at the story on the page below. Fill in the blanks on this page with the words called for. Then, using the words you have selected, fill in the blank spaces in the story.

Now you've created your own hilarious MAD LIBS® game!

GIANTS LEGENDS: BARRY BONDS

ADJECTIVE _____

NOUN _____

NOUN _____

ADJECTIVE _____

PLURAL NOUN _____

ADJECTIVE _____

NOUN _____

NOUN _____

EXCLAMATION _____

ANIMAL (PLURAL) _____

PLURAL NOUN _____

NUMBER _____

ADJECTIVE _____

PLURAL NOUN _____

VERB _____

TYPE OF FOOD _____

NOUN _____

MAD LIBS®
GIANTS LEGENDS:
BARRY BONDS

Is Barry Bonds the greatest signing in the history of _____ agency?

ADJECTIVE

Let's discuss. Bonds won the Most Valuable _____ Award five

NOUN

times over fifteen years in San Francisco. During that time, he became

baseball's _____ king, breaking Hank Aaron's _____

NOUN · ADJECTIVE

record while also compiling over 1,400 _____ batted

PLURAL NOUN

in. Oftentimes, _____ opposing pitchers refused to throw

ADJECTIVE

him a/an _____, choosing instead to issue an intentional

NOUN

_____. Fans taunted them by hollering _____

NOUN · EXCLAMATION

and symbolically waving rubber _____. Barry's at-bats

ANIMAL (PLURAL)

kept everyone glued to their _____. Even if you had to

PLURAL NOUN

go number _____ really badly, you held it because he might

NUMBER

do something _____! TV stations would even interrupt

ADJECTIVE

their scheduled _____ so viewers could watch Bonds

PLURAL NOUN

_____. Around the Bay, Barry is the son of Giants great

VERB

Bobby Bonds who proves that the _____ didn't fall far from

TYPE OF FOOD

the _____!

NOUN

MAD LIBS® is fun to play with friends, but you can also play it by yourself! To begin with, DO NOT look at the story on the page below. Fill in the blanks on this page with the words called for. Then, using the words you have selected, fill in the blank spaces in the story.

Now you've created your own hilarious MAD LIBS® game!

SOOOOO CLOSE!

NOUN _____

NOUN _____

PART OF THE BODY (PLURAL) _____

PLURAL NOUN _____

VERB _____

NOUN _____

LETTER OF THE ALPHABET _____

NOUN _____

NOUN _____

ADJECTIVE _____

SILLY WORD _____

ADJECTIVE _____

NOUN _____

ADJECTIVE _____

TYPE OF FOOD _____

NOUN _____

PART OF THE BODY _____

A PLACE _____

MAD LIBS

SOOOOO CLOSE!

Before their impossible _____ finally came true in 2010,

NOUN

the Giants often caught a whiff of the ultimate _____

NOUN

before having it slip through their _____. Twice

PART OF THE BODY (PLURAL)

they racked up 103 _____ during a season only to see

PLURAL NOUN

another team _____ the Commissioner's _____ in

VERB .... NOUN

October. In 1989, they met the Oakland _____'s in

LETTER OF THE ALPHABET

what was nicknamed the "Bay _____ Series" and the "Battle

NOUN

of the _____." Unfortunately, they were no match for their

NOUN

neighbors and the _____ duo known as the "_____

ADJECTIVE .... SILLY WORD

Brothers." The Giants returned to the Fall Classic in 2002, the first

edition to feature two _____ Card winners. They dropped the

ADJECTIVE

seventh _____ and again came home _____-handed

NOUN .... ADJECTIVE

while Dusty Baker's mischievous young son was nearly flattened like

a/an _____ by a sliding J.T. _____. You turn

TYPE OF FOOD .... NOUN

your _____ for one second and your kid wanders out to

PART OF THE BODY

(the) _____!

A PLACE

MAD LIBS® is fun to play with friends, but you can also play it by yourself! To begin with, DO NOT look at the story on the page below. Fill in the blanks on this page with the words called for. Then, using the words you have selected, fill in the blank spaces in the story.

Now you've created your own hilarious MAD LIBS® game!

HOMETOWN HERO: BRANDON CRAWFORD

A PLACE _____

ANIMAL (PLURAL) _____

PART OF THE BODY _____

ADJECTIVE _____

OCCUPATION _____

NOUN _____

PLURAL NOUN _____

A PLACE _____

NOUN _____

NOUN _____

VERB _____

ANIMAL _____

PLURAL NOUN _____

ADJECTIVE _____

PLURAL NOUN _____

ADJECTIVE _____

ADJECTIVE _____

PLURAL NOUN _____

MAD LIBS
HOMETOWN HERO:
BRANDON CRAWFORD

Your chances of playing for your beloved Giants are about the

same as (the) _____ freezing over while _____
                 A PLACE   ANIMAL (PLURAL)

fly out of your _____, but no one told that to Brandon
                 PART OF THE BODY

Crawford. In 1992, Crawford was five years old and the Giants

were on _____ ground in San Francisco. In need of a new
          ADJECTIVE

_____ with enough _____ in the bank to pay for
 OCCUPATION   NOUN

the team's _____, many believed they would move to
            PLURAL NOUN

(the) _____. That September, the local _____ showed
       A PLACE   NOUN

a picture of young Brandon standing beside a/an _____
                                                  NOUN

begging his heroes not to _____. Perhaps partially convinced
                           VERB

by the boy's sad _____ eyes, the Giants changed their
                  ANIMAL

_____. Amazingly, Crawford grew up _____
 PLURAL NOUN   ADJECTIVE

enough to become the Giants' shortstop! With two World Series

_____ and millions of _____ fans, he has altered
 PLURAL NOUN   ADJECTIVE

team history in two separate decades, proving that _____
                                                     ADJECTIVE

things can happen when you follow your _____!
                                         PLURAL NOUN

MAD LIBS® is fun to play with friends, but you can also play it by yourself! To begin with, DO NOT look at the story on the page below. Fill in the blanks on this page with the words called for. Then, using the words you have selected, fill in the blank spaces in the story.

Now you've created your own hilarious MAD LIBS® game!

MORE FAN FAVORITES

NOUN _____

SILLY WORD _____

ADJECTIVE _____

ANIMAL _____

PART OF THE BODY _____

PLURAL NOUN _____

PLURAL NOUN _____

A PLACE _____

ADJECTIVE _____

PART OF THE BODY _____

NOUN _____

MAD LIBS®

MORE FAN FAVORITES

Joe Panik: This second baseman started his Major League career with a bang by making a/an _____-saving play in the World Series.

NOUN

Kelby Tomlinson: With his signature glasses, some wonder if this mild-mannered utility player is from the planet _____, hiding

SILLY WORD
a secret identity as _____-man!

ADJECTIVE

Brandon Belt: Fans have nicknamed this popular first baseman the "Baby _____" for his long _____ and they voted

ANIMAL PART OF THE BODY
him into the All-Star Game in 2016.

Tim Lincecum: Nicknamed "The Freak" for generating incredible _____ while weighing just 170 _____, this four-

PLURAL NOUN PLURAL NOUN
time All-Star remains a beloved figure in (the) _____.

A PLACE

Johnny Cueto: With his _____ delivery and distinct

ADJECTIVE
_____-style, Cueto has become a/an _____ on

PART OF THE BODY NOUN
the pitching staff.

MAD LIBS® is fun to play with friends, but you can also play it by yourself! To begin with, DO NOT look at the story on the page below. Fill in the blanks on this page with the words called for. Then, using the words you have selected, fill in the blank spaces in the story.

Now you've created your own hilarious MAD LIBS® game!

LONG LIVE
THE CRAZY CRAB

PERSON IN ROOM _____

SILLY WORD _____

EXCLAMATION _____

NOUN _____

PLURAL NOUN _____

ADJECTIVE _____

ADJECTIVE _____

PART OF THE BODY _____

PLURAL NOUN _____

COLOR _____

ANIMAL _____

PLURAL NOUN _____

NOUN _____

NOUN _____

TYPE OF LIQUID _____

PLURAL NOUN _____

ADJECTIVE _____

ADJECTIVE _____

His theme song was more annoying than _____ singing
<u>PERSON IN ROOM</u>

Lady _____ on karaoke. Fans scornfully yelled _____
<u>SILLY WORD</u>   <u>EXCLAMATION</u>

when he was introduced. Management reinforced his costume with

a steel _____ because players threw _____ at him.
<u>NOUN</u>   <u>PLURAL NOUN</u>

He was the "_____ Crab," a crustacean so _____
<u>ADJECTIVE</u>   <u>ADJECTIVE</u>

that manager Frank Robinson wanted to flatten him with a/an

_____ sandwich! In 1984, the team was like the Island of
<u>PART OF THE BODY</u>

Misfit _____ from *Rudolph the* _____-nosed
<u>PLURAL NOUN</u>   <u>COLOR</u>

_____, and the swirling _____ at Candlestick Park
<u>ANIMAL</u>   <u>PLURAL NOUN</u>

had fans feeling irked. "Crazy Crab" was designed to be their verbal

punching _____ and mock other mascots. Insane? Yes. But it
<u>NOUN</u>

worked until rival Padres players actually cleaned his _____,
<u>NOUN</u>

sending him back to the murky _____ he swam in from.
<u>TYPE OF LIQUID</u>

Today, a new mascot leads cable _____ in parades down Market
<u>PLURAL NOUN</u>

Street and dances to "_____ Birthday" at parties, proving that
<u>ADJECTIVE</u>

Giants fans are not too _____ for mascots after all.
<u>ADJECTIVE</u>

MAD LIBS® is fun to play with friends, but you can also play it by yourself! To begin with, DO NOT look at the story on the page below. Fill in the blanks on this page with the words called for. Then, using the words you have selected, fill in the blank spaces in the story.

Now you've created your own hilarious MAD LIBS® game!

MEET THE SKIPPER: BRUCE BOCHY

A PLACE _____

NOUN _____

VERB _____

ADJECTIVE _____

PLURAL NOUN _____

ADJECTIVE _____

PLURAL NOUN _____

PART OF THE BODY _____

NOUN _____

NOUN _____

ADJECTIVE _____

NOUN _____

ADJECTIVE _____

PLURAL NOUN _____

PLURAL NOUN _____

PLURAL NOUN _____

PART OF THE BODY _____

ARTICLE OF CLOTHING _____

Bruce Bochy is the first-ever manager born in (the) _____,
                                                    A PLACE

and he managed the rival San Diego Padres before moving up the

Pacific _____ Highway. With his never-say-_____
           NOUN   VERB

attitude and ability to stay _____ under pressure, the Giants'
                                ADJECTIVE

success begins with him. An active leader in _____ as a
                                                PLURAL NOUN

manager, Bochy keeps a/an _____ demeanor while also taking
                             ADJECTIVE

no _____ from anyone. Whether in a blowout game or
     PLURAL NOUN

a/an _____-biter, his _____ remains expressionless,
       PART OF THE BODY   NOUN

often surveying the _____ through his signature shades
                        NOUN

on _____ days. When the Giants are stuck between a/an
     ADJECTIVE

_____ and a/an _____ place, Bochy always has
   NOUN   ADJECTIVE

something in his bag of _____. With a voice as gruff as a
                           PLURAL NOUN

bag of _____, he inspires his team to compete like a group
          PLURAL NOUN

of _____. What is the secret to his incredible brainpower?
     PLURAL NOUN

Some credit his massive _____, which famously requires the
                           PART OF THE BODY

largest _____ size in baseball!
           ARTICLE OF CLOTHING

Download Mad Libs today!

Join the millions of Mad Libs fans creating
wacky and wonderful stories on our apps!